COLORING BOOK
FOR SELF HEALING

AFFIRMATIONS OF LOVE, GRATITUDE & FORGIVENESS

Illustrated by

Floris V. J. de Clercq

Floris V. J. de Clercq Publishing

Berlin

Floris V. J. de Clercq Publishing

Berlin

Coloring Book Series

Coloring Book For Self Healing
Affirmations of Love, Gratitude and Forgiveness

© 2015 by Floris V. J. de Clercq

Created & illustrated by Floris V. J. de Clercq
Layout by Sebastian Märker

ISBN: 978-3-945898-03-1

For more publications, coloring books & designs by Floris V. J. de Clercq please visit
www.florisdeclercq.com

Introduction

Through more than 20 years of working in complementary therapies and self-awareness coaching it has been clear to me that the thoughts, ideas and beliefs that we focus on influence our physical health, how we feel about ourselves and how we experience and interpret our reality.

I believe that a mind filled with love, forgiveness and gratitude is a perfect environment for wholeness and well-being. An effective way of achieving this state of mind is by tapping into our playful creativity - in whatever form - whilst focusing on self-empowering thoughts and feelings.

Through my own personal journey, I have realized the benefits of combining affirmations with design and sacred geometry. This inspired me to create a series of coloring books to help you find that space between playfulness and mindful thoughts and feelings that will enable you to feel whole again.

Fill every design with love, and let each of them remind you of how amazing you are.

You are loved

Floris V. J. de Clercq

IN STILLNESS I AM PRESENT AS THE WHOLENESS OF BEING

"I Am Present" Design by Floris V.J. de Clercq   Colored by ....

I AM A WINNER! I ALLOW LOVE! I ALLOW LOVE! I LOVE LIFE! I AM GRATEFUL.

ALLOW & LOVE LIFE! I AM GRATEFUL.

I AM LOVED!

MY LIFE IS FILLED WITH PROSPERITY.

Colored by

"Transformation & Freedom" Design by Floris V.J. de Clercq

I RECEIVE LOVE * I ALLOW LOVE * I ACCEPT LOVE * I AM LOVE * I GIVE LOVE *

"The Stillness Within" Design by Floris V.J. de Clercq

FREEDOM

FREEDOM

I AM FREE

"Freedom" Design by Floris V.J. de Clercq

Colored by ....

I AM LOVE

I ACCEPT & ALLOW TRANSFORMATION

"The Phoenix" Design by Floris V.J. de Clercq   Colored by ....

I AM LIFE   I AM LIGHT   I AM LOVE   I AM PEACE

"Tree of Love" Design by Floris U.J. de Clercq

Colored by ....

I AM EVERYTHING ✰ I AM EVERYTHING ✰

✰ I SEE EVERYTHING

STILLNESS = I AM
STILLNESS = I AM
STILLNESS = I AM

IN STILLNESS, I AM THE SINGLE EYE ✰

"Awakening the 3rd Eye" Design by Floris V.J. de Clercq

Colored by

MY THOUGHTS & BELIEFS INFLUENCE THE REALITY I PERCEIVE. I CHOOSE LOVE.

I AM LOVE. I AM LOVED. I GIVE LOVE UNCONDITIONALLY. I RECEIVE LOVE UNCONDITIONALLY. I AM LIGHT, LIFE & LOVE.

"Flowers for Brains" Design by Floris V.J. de Clercq   Colored by ....

EVERY CELL IN MY BODY IS FILLED WITH LIGHT, LIFE AND LOVE

"Light" Design by Floris V.J. de Clercq

Colored by ....

FORGIVENESS=GRATITUDE

I FORGIVE MYSELF—I FORGIVE YOU

FORGIVENESS
GRATITUDE
LOVE

I FORGIVE MYSELF—I FORGIVE YOU

GRATITUDE
FORGIVENESS
LOVE

GRATITUDE=FORGIVENESS

Colored by

Forgiveness = Gratitude" Design by Floris V.J. de Clercq

"I Am Love" Design by Floris V.J. de Clercq

Colored by ....

I AM FREE FREE FREE I AM FREE I AM FREEDOM I AM FREEDOM FREEDOM

Awakening to Freedom" Design by Floris V.J. de Clercq

Colored by ....

Colored by

ABUNDANCE I ALLOW WELL-BEING

I ALLOW SUCCESSFUL IN EVERYTHING I DO. I ALLOW WEALTH, PROSPERITY & ABUNDANCE TO FLOW EFFORTLESSLY INTO MY LIFE. I AM HEALTHY WHOLE & RADIANT. I AM

I ALLOW WEALTH

I ALLOW PROSPERITY I ALLOW

"Wholeness" Design by Floris V.J. de Clercq   Colored by ....

I GIVE LOVE

I RECEIVE LOVE

I GIVE LOVE

Colored by

"A Colorful Life" Design by Floris V.J. de Clercq

I AM LOVE

THE POWER IS WITHIN ME TO CHOOSE AN ABUNDANT, PROSPEROUS, JOYFUL & LOVING LIFE. I LOVE MY LIFE. I EXUDE LOVE. I LOVE MY WORLD. THE POWER IS WITHIN ME. I CAN ACHIEVE ANYTHING. THE POWER IS WITHIN ME TO CHOOSE AN ABUNDANT, PROSPEROUS, JOYFUL & LOVING LIFE. I AM LOVE. I CAN ACHIEVE ANYTHING. WHOLENESS & GRATITUDE.

I AM LOVE

"Flower of Love" Design by Floris V.J. de Clercq   Colored by ....

Text within the central circular design: **UNCONDITIONAL LOVE = HEAVEN ON EARTH**

"Holographic Reality" Design by Floris V.J. de Clercq   Colored by ....

WELL-BEING, WEALTH, ABUNDANCE, JOY & PROSPERITY FLOW THROUGH ME, ALLOWING ME TO CREATE A FULFILLING LIFE ☆ I LOVE WHO & WHAT I AM. I AM FILLED WITH GRATITUDE & LOVE. I AM GRATEFUL FOR MY WELL-BEING, WEALTH & PROSPERITY ☆

"Choice—A Blue Print" Design by Floris V.J. de Clercq   Colored by ....

I HAVE A WONDERFUL JOYFUL LIFE

I RADIATE LOVE ☆ I HAVE A

☆ I RECEIVE LOVE ☆

I GIVE LOVE ☆

I AM LOVED ☆

I AM LOVED ☆ I AM LOVE ☆ I LOVE MY WORLD ☆ I LOVE MY LIFE ☆ I LOVE MY LIFE

I LOVE MY LIFE

"Tree of Life" Design by Floris V.J. de Clercq

Colored by

I FORGIVE MYSELF FOR JUDGING OTHERS

"Forgiveness" Design by Floris V.J. de Clercq

Colored by ....

"Love Dragon" Design by Floris V.J. de Clercq   Colored by ....

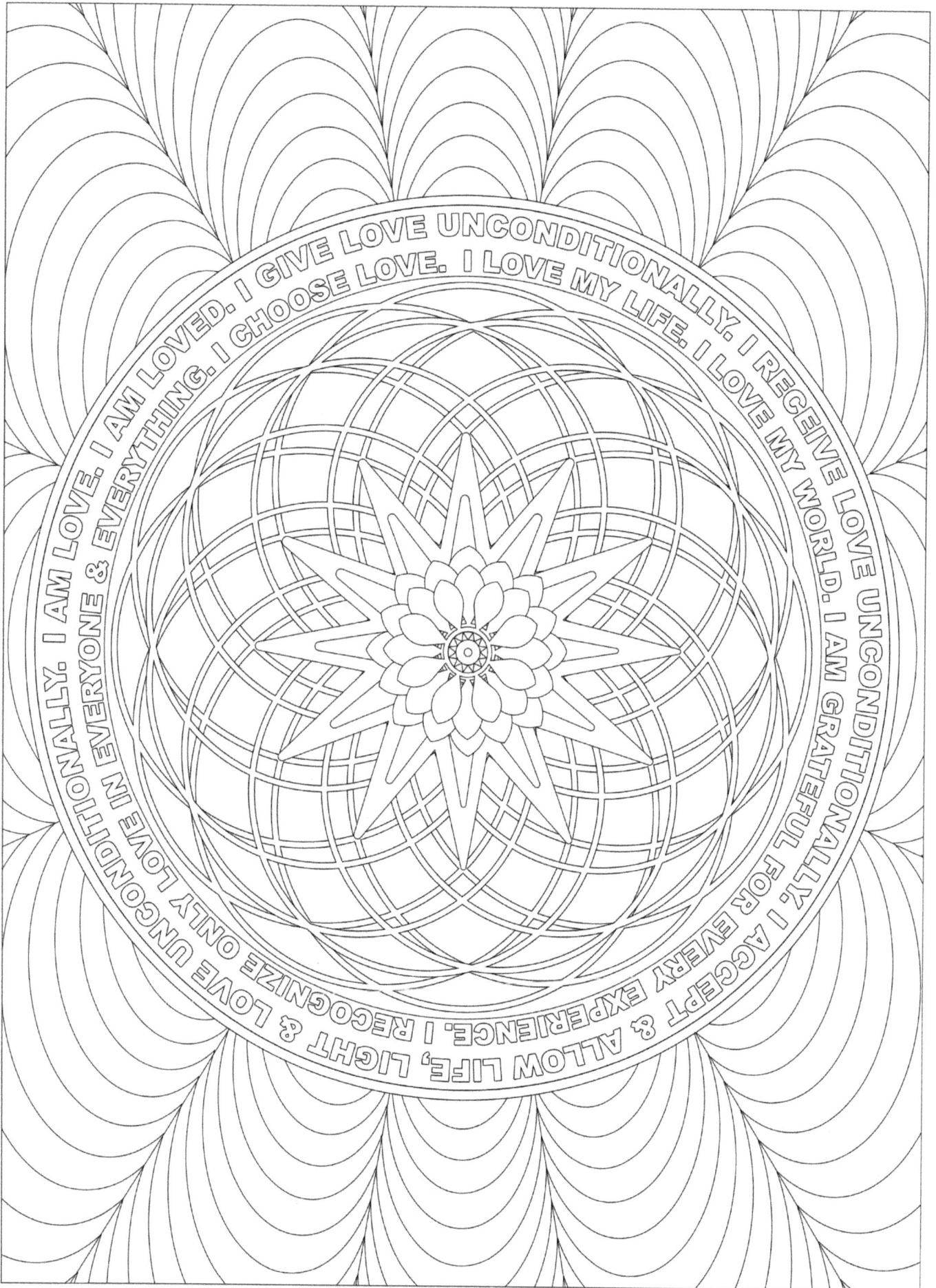

I GIVE LOVE UNCONDITIONALLY. I RECEIVE LOVE UNCONDITIONALLY. I AM GRATEFUL FOR EVERY EXPERIENCE. I RECOGNIZE ONLY LOVE IN EVERYONE & EVERYTHING. I CHOOSE LOVE. I LOVE MY LIFE. I LOVE MY WORLD. I AM GRATEFUL. I ACCEPT & ALLOW LIFE, LIGHT & LOVE UNCONDITIONALLY IN EVERYONE & EVERYTHING. I AM LOVE. I AM LOVED.

"Love—Allow" Design by Floris V.J. de Clercq   Colored by ....

"I Receive Love" Design by Floris V.J. de Clercq

Colored by _____

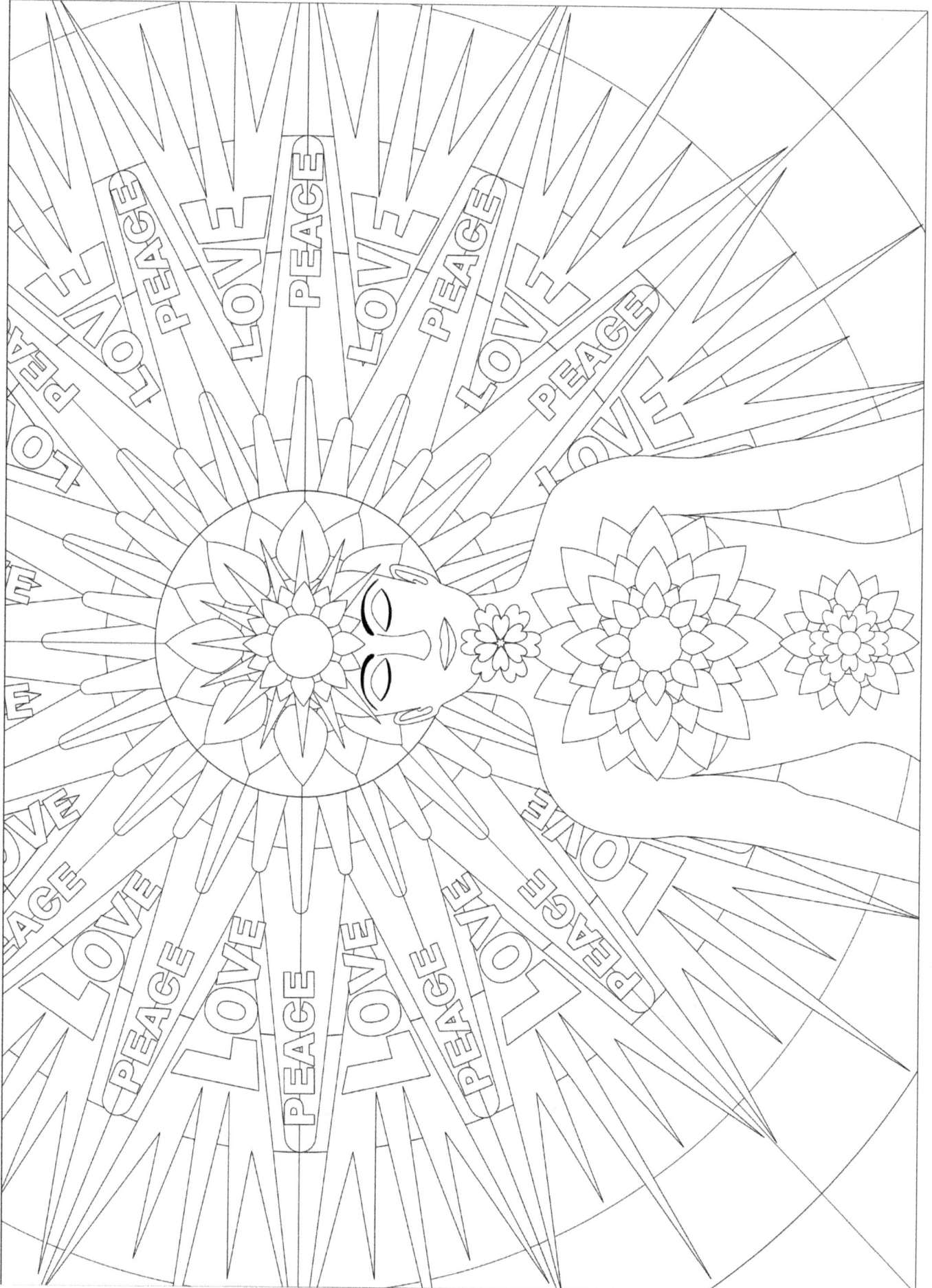

"Enlightenment" Design by Floris V.J. de Clercq

Colored by ....

I HAVE INFINITE LOVE
I HAVE LOVED   I HAVE LOVE
I AM LOVED
I HAVE LOVE
I HAVE LOVE
I HAVE LOVE
I AM LOVE
I AM LOVE
I AM LOVE
I AM LOVE

I RECOGNIZE INFINITE LOVE IN EVERYONE
I RECOGNIZE INFINITE LOVE IN EVERYONE

"Recognize Love" Design by Floris V.J. de Clercq   Colored by ....

I AM LOVE • I AM LOVED • I AM LIFE • I HAVE LOVE • I LOVE LIFE • I LOVE • I AM LOVE • I AM LOVED • I AM LIFE • I HAVE LOVE • I LOVE LIFE

"I Have Love" Design by Floris V.J. de Clercq   Colored by

Mandala text (clockwise from top): I AM LOVE * I AM LOVED * I HAVE LOVE * I GIVE LOVE * I RECEIVE LOVE * I AM JOY * I HAVE JOY * I AM GRATEFUL * I AM LOVE * I AM * I LOVE MY LIFE * I LOVE MY WORLD *

Inner petals: LOVE

"Love" Design by Floris V.J. de Clercq

Colored by

"A Slice of Love" Design by Floris V.J. de Clercq   Colored by ....

For more publications, coloring books & designs by
Floris V. J. de Clercq please visit
www.florisdeclercq.com

Floris V. J. de Clercq Publishing

Berlin

www.ingramcontent.com/pod-product-compliance
Lightning Source LLC
Chambersburg PA
CBHW081152040426
42445CB00015B/1848